JOE BEEF

JOE BEEF

(A History of Pointe Saint Charles)

David Fennario

Talonbooks • Vancouver • 1991

Published with assistance from the Canada Council.

Talonbooks
201 - 1019 East Cordova Street
Vancouver
British Columbia V6A 1M8
Canada

This book was designed by Sally Bryer Mennell, typeset in 10/12
point Palacio by Pièce de Résistance Ltée., and printed in Canada
by Hignell Printing Ltd.

First printing: September 1991.

Canadian Cataloguing in Publication Data

Fennario, David, 1947 –
  Joe Beef

  ISBN 0-88922-291-6

  I. Title.
PS8561.E54J6 1991   C812'.54   C91-091488-5
PR9199.3.F45J6 1991

JOE BEEF was originally produced by the Black Rock Community Group in Montreal, Quebec, with the following cast:

Joe Beef	Georges Beriault
Worker, Soldier, McTavish, Bloke, MacDonald, Louis Cyr, Pink Lady	Nelson Calder
Voice, Chief Pegus, Habitant, Worker, Papineau, Smith, Irish Woman	Mary Fraser
Mickey, Worker, Habitant, Bucheron, Lucky Lady	Virgil Clampett Keyes
McGill, Habitant, Worker, Soldier, Patriote Irish Woman	Susann Leger
Habitant, Soldier, Molson, Bucheron, Worker, Blue Lady	Jay Lichacz
Indian, Soldier, Worker, McGillivray, Durham, Doctor, Abbott	Dean Neiderer
Worker, Indian, Habitant, Voyageur, Patriote, Kelly, Mother Superior, Irish Woman	Sandra Robinson
Woman, Habitant, Voyageur, Patriote, Worker, Irish Woman	Paya Rohay
Capitalist, Seigneur Daversiere, Worker, Voyageur, Ogilvie, Lord Gosford, Prince	Johnny Salmela
Soldier, General, Simpson, Bloke, Brassey, Redpath, Percival, Irish Woman	Sheila Salmela
Priest, Griffin, Sir John, Hugh Allan	Jim Sorley
Worker, Jenny the Bear	Richard White

Directed by David Fennario. Set design by Sheila Salmela and Dean Neiderer. Lighting by Gary Elson, Mary Fraser and Barclay Watt.

A second performance of *JOE BEEF* was done by Mixed Company at Harbourfront in Toronto, with the following cast:

Chorus Bucheron	Sean Baker
Seigneur, Gosford, Gompers	Allen Booth
Chorus Irish Woman	Laurie Bowker
McTavish, Sir Hugh Allan	Steven Bush
McGill, Lepine	Jennifer Dean
John Molson, Abbott	Mary Durkan
Joe Beef	John Friesen
Priest, Sir John, Bourget	Michael Glassbourg
Papineau, Darlington	Nancy Hindmarsh
Chorus Chief Pegus	Eileen O'Toole

Directed by Simon Malbogat. Music by Allen Booth. Choreography by Margaret Dragu. Set Design by Hersh Jacob. Costume and Props design by L.W. Foden. Lighting by Jim Plaxton.

CHARACTERS

Joe Beef
Seigneur
Priest
General
McGill
McTavish
Molson
Chief Pegus
McGillivray
Simpson
Allan
Gentleman
Doctor
Abbott
Darlington
Lepine
Gompers
Bourget
Cast 1-7
Habitants 1-3
Soldiers
Voyageurs 1-2
Woman 1-3
Bourgeois 1-2
Workers 1-4
Nuns

Because the play was written for performance in clubs, schools, small halls, as well as theatres, the set requirements are simple and portable. A bar with bottles and glasses for Joe Beef, along with a replica of the Black Rock memorial stone that was placed on the common grave of the 6,000 Irish immigrants who died of typhoid fever in Pointe Saint Charles back in the time of the great famine of 1844-47 in Ireland.

Other props consist of hockey sticks painted black, walking canes, top hats, cocked hats and various costumes designed so that the cast members playing multiple roles can change rapidly in between scenes.

Lighting can be simple or ambitious, depending on available resources. The main visual impact is in the costumes.

Most of the show is performed straight to the audience in one way or another, with each of the cast members playing multiple roles. The show has been done with a minimum of eight and a maximum of twenty-one. Because of the lack of female roles, we always had some of the women in the cast play male roles.

*JOE BEEF in a tavern apron serving beer from
behind his bar in the working class district of Pointe
Saint Charles in Montreal, Quebec.*

JOE BEEF:
Last call, last call for alcohol.

*Serves the last beers to the audience members while
the cast mingle around the bar and put on their
Molson baseball hats.*

Last call.

He guzzles down a beer.

Going—going—gone. Ah, showtime, showtime . . .
hey, come on, line up and introduce yourselves.

*The CAST, dressed in black, line up facing the
audience.*

JOE BEEF:
And I know this is a hard question, but what's your
names and where are ya from?

*CAST members give their names, place of birth and
then greet the audience with their arms out and a
step forward in unison.*

CAST:
And we're all here in person.

JOE BEEF:
Joe Beef's the name
And beer's the game
I've got this joint
Down here in the Pointe
Home of the steame'e all dressed to go
The Frogs, the Pepsis and the Blokes

The CAST still standing in line facing the audience.

CAST 1:
> Tabarnac

CAST 2:
> Calice

CAST 3:
> Ostie

JOE BEEF: *pointing at a member of the audience*
> Hey, tête cawrey, don't fuck with me.

CAST 4:
> Where casse croute's serve the patates frites

CAST 5:
> And chienchaud Pogo's on a stick

CAST 6:
> Where fried baloney on a plate

CAST: *together*
> Is what we call Mulroney Steak

CAST 1:
> Where TV night is black and white

CAST 2:
> Get married if you want to fight

CAST 3:
> Hey Joe, I'm waiting for my cheque

CAST 4:
> I need four bucks for cigarettes

CAST 5:
> And puff-puff-puff

CAST 6:
> Drink-drink-drink

CAST 7:
> Dirty dishes in the sink

CAST 1:
> Got no credit

CAST 2:
> Got no cash

CAST 3:
> The baby's sick

CAST 4:
> He's got a rash

CAST 7:
> I'll sell my shoes

JOE BEEF:
> For a bottle of booze

CAST: *together*
> When I got the Welfare Blues

> > *JOE BEEF steps out into center stage and leads the cast in a song-and-dance routine.*

JOE BEEF: *singing in a simple chanting tone*
> Now things down here in Pointe Saint Charles
> Are enough to make you sick
> Your ceiling's falling down
> And your toilet's full of shit
> But don't call the landlord
> And don't fight City Hall
> 'Cause even if you try it
> You'll never win at all

CAST: *together*
> So have another brew, have another brew
> 'Cause nothing's gonna turn out right no matter
> what you do
> So have another brew, have another brew

'Cause nothing's gonna turn out right
No matter what you do

JOE BEEF:
And all you welfare mothers
Waiting for your cheques
Don't worry about the children
And forget about the rent
Just sit down, relax yourself
And have another brew
'Cause nothing's gonna work out right
No matter what you do

CAST: *together*
No matter what you do
No matter what you do
So sit down, relax yourself
And have another brew
Have another brew, have another brew
'Cause nothing's gonna turn out right
No matter what you do

JOE BEEF:
And all you workers
That want to go on strike
'Cause you want a better living
You want a better life
But don't walk a picket line
And don't put up a fight
'Cause striking is illegal —
You don't have any rights

CAST: *together*
So have another brew, have another brew
Just sit down, relax yourself and have another brew
Have another brew, have another brew
'Cause nothing's gonna turn out right no matter
what you do

> *The CAST turns and exits left and right, still
> singing the chorus as JOE BEEF steps back to his bar.*

JOE BEEF:

> Thank you, Molson Dancers, yeah, yeah, yeah.
> Nothing's gonna turn out right no matter what you
> do. And ya talk to people around here and that's the
> way they feel, right? They figure, well, that's the way
> things are and that's the way it's always been. But
> it's not true. I mean there have been times when
> people did try to do something about the shit we're
> living in down here and I ought to know 'cause I've
> been around as long as there's been a Pointe Saint
> Charles and I can remember when there was no
> welfare. I can remember when you guys were trying
> to form your first goddamn unions and ya know
> what? Ya made a lot of mistakes and ya know
> something else? You're still making the same stupid
> fucking mistakes . . . otherwise ya never would have
> voted a guy like Bourassa back into power. I mean,
> don't ya remember what he did to you last time? No,
> ya don't. Ya don't remember and I know you'll
> probably forget this by tomorrow morning, but
> tonight we're gonna tell ya something about
> yourselves. We're gonna tell ya all about the history
> of Pointe Saint Charles. Oh yeah, you got a history
> too, but it's not the one you seen on TV or flunked
> in high school. No, this is the real story, the true
> story of what you did and did not do, beginning
> away, away back, with that first mistake, when, the
> Seigneur de la Daversiere, Boulevard.

> *SEIGNEUR enters dressed with fancy cocked hat*
> *with a fur pelt and a pistol stuck in his sash.*

SEIGNEUR:

> That's me.

JOE BEEF:

> Meet Polyvalente, Jean Jacques Olier.

> *PRIEST enters in black robe carrying bible and*
> *crucifix.*

13

PRIEST:
>That's me.

JOE BEEF:
>Who, after having a dream that the Island of
>Montreal was to be consecrated to the Holy Family
>were both "on a sudden enlightened by a heavenly
>and extraordinary gleam."

>>*JOE BEEF makes a tinkling sound by banging a
>>stirring spoon against a bottle as the PRIEST and
>>SEIGNEUR both look up at the sky.*

PRIEST:
>Extraordinaire.

SEIGNEUR:
>Extraordinaire.

>>*They look at each other.*

SEIGNEUR and PRIEST:
>You are having the same dream?

SEIGNEUR: *looking at the audience*
>Money.

PRIEST: *looking at the audience*
>Montréal.

SEIGNEUR:
>Money.

PRIEST:
>We must go there and build a temple to the Lord.

SEIGNEUR:
>Oui, and a fort too, heh? Just in case — I mean, the
>Lord helps those that help themselves — heh?

>>*He slaps at a mosquito.*

Crisse, these mosquitos.

PRIEST:

> Yes, we must convert our red brethren here to the Christian faith and save their souls. There's one over there.

SEIGNEUR: *aims his pistol and shoots*
BOOM.

> *We hear a painful groan as the PRIEST makes the sign of the cross and the SEIGNEUR blows smoke away from his pistol.*

SEIGNEUR:

> Oui, save some souls and some sous too, heh? Hey, they're making big bucks out of those buckskins, big bucks.

> *He pulls his fur pelt out of his sash.*

PRIEST:

> I must speak to the Bishop about forming a new Seminary. How does the Seminary of Saint Sulpice sound to you?

SEIGNEUR:

> Saint Sul-piss? How does the Company of One Hundred Associates sound to you? I mean, I know ninety-nine other guys who, they're interested too, I mean, in saving the souls of those red brothers there.

> *He points his pistol and fires.*

BOOM.

> *Another groan of pain as the PRIEST makes the sign of the cross.*

SEIGNEUR:

> Hey push off! We're claiming this island in the name of the Blessed Holy Mother.

PRIEST: *waving away the mosquitos*
Let us pray.

SEIGNEUR:
Pray? But a short one, heh Father? The bugs are bad.

The SEIGNEUR gets on his knees slapping away at the bugs.

PRIEST:
Almighty Father we offer our Thanksgiving on this, our first Mass of our mission here in Ville Marie de Montréal, on May the Eighteenth Anno Domini 1642.

SEIGNEUR:
BOOM.

There is another painful groan.

PRIEST:
Hear us, O Lord, and bless us.

SEIGNEUR:
Bless us.

SEIGNEUR makes the sign of the cross as he gets up off his knees with eyes wary for Iroquois.

PRIEST: *raising his arms to heaven*
"We are but a grain of mustard seed that shall rise and grow till its branches overshadow the earth. We are few, but our work is the work of God. His smile is upon us and our children shall fill the land."

SEIGNEUR:
Fill the land.

SEIGNEUR and PRIEST:
Fill the land.

Both the PRIEST and the SEIGNEUR raise their arms.

SEIGNEUR and PRIEST:
>Avancez les Peasoups.

>>*HABITANTS enter carrying hockey sticks being used as farm tools in this scene. They are wearing sashes and tuques.*

HABITANT 1: *singing to the tune of "Frère Jacques"*
>Chop that wood, chop that wood

HABITANTS 2 and 3:
>Cut that hay, cut that hay

HABITANT 1:
>I want to quit it

HABITANTS 2 and 3:
>I'm sick of mud and shit

HABITANTS: *together*
>Tabarnac, Tabarnac

HABITANT 1:
>Pain in the h'ass, pain in the h'ass

HABITANTS 2 and 3:
>A sore back too, a sore back too

HABITANT 1:
>We came for milk and honey

HABITANTS 2 and 3:
>But the Seigneur takes our money.

SEIGNEUR and PRIEST:
>But God loves you, God loves you

PRIEST:
>God-Is-Love

JOE BEEF: *standing at his bar*
>But meanwhile the habitants must give one-tenth of

all they produce to the Church and the Seigneur;
one-tenth of their wood, their fish, their wheat.

HABITANTS: *together*
And we must work on our Seigneur's land for free.

SEIGNEUR:
Hey, hey, the Meek shall inherit the earth okay? So
don't worry about it, right Father?

PRIEST:
That's right my children. God wants you to suffer
because He loves you.

HABITANT 1:
I wish He didn't love us so much.

SEIGNEUR:
Hey, okay, what's your names anyhow?

HABITANTS: *together*
Our names?

SEIGNEUR:
Oui, your names. We got to know your names.

HABITANTS: *together*
Joe.

SEIGNEUR:
Crisse, you're all named Joe?

HABITANTS: *together*
Oui.

PRIEST:
Very well, okay les Joes, down on your knees.

SEIGNEUR:
Down on your knees.

The HABITANTS get down on their knees.

PRIEST: *his hands together in prayer*
Oh Lord, please accept these Peasoups as members
of the Holy Mother Church.

SEIGNEUR:
Amen.

PRIEST:
And from now on let them be known by their new
Christian names as I now baptize you, Joe
Une. *(makes the sign of the cross over JOE UNE)* Joe
Deux . . . *(makes the sign of the cross over JOE
DEUX)* puis Joe Trois . . . *(makes the sign of the cross
over JOE TROIS.)*

HABITANT 1:
Joe Une?

HABITANT 2:
Joe Deux?

HABITANT 3:
Joe Trois?

SEIGNEUR:
Yes . . . yes and your name is also your new social
insurance number and don't forget it.

PRIEST:
And now rise and sing-sing.

> *The HABITANTS get off their knees and exit singing
> "God is Love" to the tune of the Volga Boatmen's
> song.*

HABITANTS:
God is Love . . . huh . . . God is
Love . . . huh . . . love love love love . . . God is
Love . . . huh.

JOE BEEF: *standing at his bar*
Oh yeah, God certainly did smile on the Seminary of

Saint Sulpice who now own millions and millions of dollars worth of real estate here in Quebec. Which is not bad for a bunch of guys dedicated to Faith, Hope . . .

PRIEST:

Puis la Charité.

SEIGNEUR:

And what's a little beaver to you, heh? Something on the back of a nickel? Something between the legs of a girl? No, my friends, believe me, it's money, bucks, buckskins *(holds up the buckskins)* and phee-you, they smell, they stink but it's the smell of money my friends: six millions de livres in the year of 1696 alone.

PRIEST:

Six million de livres?

SEIGNEUR:

Six million, my friend.

PRIEST:

Oh.

SEIGNEUR:

Oh.

PRIEST:

Oh.

> *They link arms and begin singing ''We Got Money'' to the tune of ''Alouette.''*

SEIGNEUR and PRIEST:

We got money, we got lots of money
We got money, we got lots of dough

PRIEST:

We got money over here

SEIGNEUR and PRIEST pointing.

SEIGNEUR:
> We got money over there

PRIEST:
> Over here

SEIGNEUR:
> Over there

PRIEST:
> Place Ville Marie

SEIGNEUR:
> La Bonaventure

SEIGNEUR and PRIEST:
> Everywhere

PRIEST:
> Oh

SEIGNEUR:
> Oh

PRIEST:
> Oh

SEIGNEUR:
> Oh

> *Sound of SOLDIERS marching offstage getting louder.*

SOLDIERS and GENERAL: *together*
> Gotta dig . . . gotta dig . . . gotta dig . . . dig . . . dig

PRIEST:
> Oh-oh?

SOLDIERS:
>Gotta dig . . . gotta dig . . . gotta dig . . . dig . . . dig

>*They continue marching. Sounds getting louder offstage.*

SEIGNEUR:
>Hey, what's that? C'est quoi ça?

PRIEST:
>It's those Squareheads, tête cawrey.

SEIGNEUR:
>Tabarnac, everytime we start to make some good money, those blokes they show up again.

>*Two soldiers enter dressed in Union Jack T-shirts carrying hockey stick rifles. They are lead by GENERAL AMHERST dressed in red coat and cocked hat. They march in place.*

JOE BEEF: *standing at his bar*
>September 1760, General Jeffery Amherst with ten thousand British regulars and colonial militia approach Ville de Montréal, camping that night outside the walls of the city in the area that would later be known as, you guessed it, Pointe Saint Charles.

GENERAL:
>Soldiers, attention.

>*SOLDIERS come to attention. The GENERAL steps up and salutes the SEIGNEUR and PRIEST who make fun of his salute.*

GENERAL:
>Very well monsieur and monseigneur, will you or will you not accept the divine right of His Gracious Majesty, King George the Third, to have sovereign dominion over the province of New France or do we have to kick the living shit out of you?

SEIGNEUR:
> Hey, we can kick some shit too, heh?

PRIEST:
> That's right, my son.

SEIGNEUR and PRIEST: *both yelling*
> Avancez les Peasoups.

> *HABITANTS enter carrying their hockey stick hoes.*

GENERAL:
> Very well — Soldiers . . . Present Arms!

> *The SOLDIERS put their hockey sticks down,*
> *prepared now to play hockey.*

SEIGNEUR:
> Very well, okay, Les Peasoups . . . Present Arms!

HABITANTS: *singing as they swing their sticks*
> Chop that wood, chop that wood

SEIGNEUR:
> No, no, not that.

> *Stops them and puts their sticks down.*

HABITANTS:
> But what do we do?

SEIGNEUR:
> Just stop the blokes from scoring, that's all.

HABITANT 1:
> Thanks a lot, boss.

HABITANT 3:
> Thanks for nothing.

SEIGNEUR:
> Hey, I got my eye on you, Joe Trois.

*The GENERAL blows his whistle and the BLOKES
and PEASOUPS start circling around thrice.
JOE BEEF starts his imitation of two hockey
commentators using a beer bottle as a microphone.*

JOE BEEF:

Good evening, hockey fans out here in Canada and
the United States and good evening Dick. Evening
Danny, well it looks like a good one tonight. — Yes,
we have two aggressive teams and we should be
seeing some good hockey. — Right Danny and I
wouldn't be surprised if we see some upsets here
tonight. — Yes the Blokes are in top form this
evening with Mad Dog Murphy and Slasher Stilman;
Slasher in top form as you can see.

*The GENERAL blows the whistle and drops the
puck.*

JOE BEEF:

It's the first period and the Blokes are moving up the
ice — the Peasoups moving back — oh, was that highsticking or was that highsticking? Elbows in the corner —
ouch, wow, what a hook, and another and another.

*The GENERAL blows the whistle stopping the
players who have been going through the movements
of the game in slow motion.*

GENERAL:

Penalty shot. The Peasoups.

JOE BEEF and SEIGNEUR and PRIEST:

The Peasoups?

SEIGNEUR and PRIEST:

Tabarnac.

JOE BEEF:

I don't want to say this on the air, Danny, but holy
good fucking shit, what a travesty of the great game
of hockey.

24

*GENERAL blows the whistle as MAD DOG
MURPHY goes down the ice for the penalty shot.*

JOE BEEF:
> And here comes Mad Dog looking a bit slow tonight
> — taking his time — but oh, watch out for Slasher
> Stilman.

> *SLASHER bumps into one of the HABITANTS
> playing goalie.*

JOE BEEF:
> Oh, he scores.

> *The BLOKES cheer.*

HABITANTS and SEIGNEUR:
> Tabarnac.

PRIEST:
> Shit — la merde.

SEIGNEUR: *throws up his hands*
> Alright, alright, okay, Crisse, I surrender, I give up.

PRIEST:
> Moi aussi.

GENERAL:
> Very well, Soldiers — Attention.

> *SOLDIERS come to attention.*

PRIEST:
> We're all gentlemen here, we're all Christians — let's
> make a deal.

SEIGNEUR:
> Oui, there's enough here for everyone.

GENERAL:
> The British Empire believes in sharing the wealth.

SEIGNEUR:

> Of course, of course, how much do you want?

GENERAL:

> The British Empire also believes in fair play. It's not whether you win or lose, it's how you play the game.

SOLDIERS:

> Hear! Hear!

SEIGNEUR:

> Oui-oui. How much do you want?

GENERAL:

> All the fur trade and the cities. You can keep the land.

SEIGNEUR:

> All the furs?

GENERAL:

> Yes.

SEIGNEUR:

> Even the squirrels?

GENERAL:

> Even the bloody chipmunks.

SEIGNEUR:

> Calice.

PRIEST:

> And the Church?

GENERAL:

> The British Empire also believes that God is Love and we wish the Church to continue its divine mission of encouraging Obedience, Loyalty and Respect towards their betters amongst the Masses — hit that one over there.

SOLDIER hits one of the HABITANTS who is trying to pick up his tuque.

PRIEST:
> It's not such a bad deal.

SEIGNEUR:
> I don't know.

GENERAL:
> Do you wish to resume hostilities?

SEIGNEUR:
> No, no, we're not ready for overtime.

HABITANTS:
> No-No.

PRIEST:
> Where do we sign?

GENERAL pulls out a contract.

GENERAL:
> Right here.

SEIGNEUR signs and then the PRIEST.

SEIGNEUR:
> I don't like it, but I got to do it, heh?

PRIEST:
> That's right, my son.

GENERAL:
> At least we're not American.

PRIEST:
> Yes, uh, do you mind General, if we just name a street after you? Rue Amherst? We're running out of boulevards.

GENERAL:
> Rue Amherst will do quite satisfactorily, thank you.

PRIEST:
> No, thank you.

> > *Cocks his nose at the GENERAL as he turns his*
> > *back. The SEIGNEUR goes up to the PEASOUPS.*

SEIGNEUR:
> Okay, les Peasoups, so this is our new boss, so that
> makes him your new boss too, tu comprends?

HABITANTS:
> Another one, calice.

SEIGNEUR:
> Oui-oui, now sing-sing.

PRIEST:
> Raise your voices to the Lord.

> > *The HABITANTS exit singing "God is Love" to the*
> > *tune of the Volga Boatmen's song.*

GENERAL:
> Eyes right!

> > *SOLIDERS turn eyes right and proceed to march off*
> > *singing.*

SOLDIERS:
> Skinflutes tight, assholes to the floor
> We're the boys that never quit
> We always ask for more
> We're the heroes of the night
> We'd rather fuck than fight
> We never ask what's wrong or right
> Cause we're the British Army

> > *They exit.*

JOE BEEF: *at his bar*
The British Empire, remember that? United Empire
Loyalists with the ''Butcher's Apron'' — the Union
Jack hanging in all the classrooms. And Wolfe dying
gallantly on the Plains of Abraham — ''Shoot me up
Gridley,'' he said or something like that. But
anyhow, the Brits soon moved into town where they
knocked down the old City walls 'cause the walls
blocked up the traffic and traffic meant trade and
trade meant money and money meant everything to
men like Simon ''The Bear'' McTavish.

> *MCTAVISH appears stage left making the sounds of*
> *a bagpipe.*

JOE BEEF:
And James ''Fool on the Hill'' McGill.

> *MCGILL appears stage right also making the sounds*
> *of a bagpipe. They are both wearing Scottish Bonnets*
> *and plaid scarves. They approach center stage*
> *singing.*

MCGILL and MCTAVISH:
The Scotties are coming — awaw — awaw
The Scotties are coming — awaw — awaw
The Scotties are coming to make some good money
The Scotties are coming — awaw — awaw

JOE BEEF: *yelling with hands up to his ears*
Somebody kill that cat.

> *MCGILL and MCTAVISH stand together at center*
> *stage facing the audience.*

MCGILL:
And the Lord God said

MCTAVISH:
And John Calvin said

MCGILL:
> And the Elders of the Presbyterian Church said

MCTAVISH:
> Accumulate

MCGILL:
> Accumulate

MCGILL and MCTAVISH:
> Accumulate

MCGILL:
> It's the will of God

MCTAVISH:
> It's Supply and Demand

MCGILL:
> It's the Law of Nature

MCTAVISH:
> The big fish eat the little fish

MCGILL:
> The little fish eat the minnows

MCTAVISH:
> The minnows eat the worms

MCGILL and MCTAVISH:
> And we eat everything

MCGILL:
> Hook

MCTAVISH:
> Line

MCGILL:
> And Sinker

They do another song and dance together.

MCGILL and MCTAVISH: *singing to the tune of "You'll Take the High Road and I'll Take the Low Road."*
>Oh you do it our way
>Or else take the highway
>'Cause we'll make the profits before ye
>For me and my partners are the Northwest Company
>And if ye think we're fooling
>Just try us and ye'll see

MCGILL:
>Aye.

MCTAVISH:
>Fucking Gr-reat.

MCGILL:
>Aye.

MCTAVISH:
>Which reminds me . . .

>*MCTAVISH takes out his spyglass and looks through it as CHIEF PEGUS in buckskins enters holding a totem mask in front of his face.*

MCGILL:
>Ye see anything yet?

MCTAVISH:
>Not yet. Hey Chief, ye seen ought of our canoes? Hey Chief?

MCGILL:
>He's deaf.

MCTAVISH:
>Deaf? Aye, when he wants to be.

>*They head over to the bar to get some drinks.*

MCGILL:

Well, they're late this year, they're really late.

MCTAVISH:

Aye, the ice broke up on the river a week ago.

MCGILL:

Who's in charge?

MCTAVISH:

My nephew, William McGillivray.

MCGILL:

Ye think they're in trouble with the boys from the Bay?

MCTAVISH:

It's hard not to think of the Bay.

MCGILL: *takes a drink*

Les Pays d'en Haut.

MCTAVISH:

Do ye miss it, James?

MCGILL:

Aye, I do.

MCTAVISH:

Setting out in the morning pulling away from the docks of Montreal.

MCGILL:

A hundred canoes all forty feet long with thirty men in every one.

MCTAVISH:

Up the river past the Lachine Rapids through Lake Ontario into Lake Erie into Lake Huron and up through Lake Superior doing nine hundred miles in less than three weeks.

32

MCGILL:
> The air, how clean the air was.

MCTAVISH:
> Les Pays d'en Haut.

MCGILL:
> The stars at night.

MCTAVISH:
> The Jack Pines.

MCGILL:
> The sparkling waters.

MCTAVISH:
> The glorious sunsets.

MCGILL:
> The bloody traps.

MCTAVISH:
> Snowblindness.

MCGILL:
> Shooting the wolves.

JOE BEEF:
> Shooting the Indians.

MCTAVISH:
> Shooting the Indians.

MCGILL:
> Aye, sometimes.

MCTAVISH:
> Fucking Gr-eat.

> *MOLSON enters dressed in bourgeois costume of top
> hat, cane, white gloves and black cape. He is also*

carrying a large black bible. He stands and addresses the
audience from center stage, across from CHIEF PEGUS.

MOLSON:

But, really, no doubt there were some Canadian fur
traders who were selfish, unreasonable and hard to
please, but, unlike our unprincipled American
cousins to the south, we consider ourselves devoted
to our red brethren. Devoted and dedicated to
bringing Civilization, Morality and Religion into the
wilderness where the grateful Indians feel themselves
bonded to their white brothers by the greatest of all
ties — Gratitude — right Chief?

CHIEF PEGUS gives MOLSON the finger.

MCTAVISH:

Bullshit.

MOLSON:

What's that, Mr. McTavish?

MCTAVISH:

To tell ye the truth, I prefer the Yankees. No guilt,
just cash.

MOLSON:

But we never sold liquor to the Indians.

MCGILL:

Not officially.

MCTAVISH:

Aye, and I'll have ye know that I've let plenty of
Indians starve outside my fort because that's the way
it is and that's the way it's got to be if we are to be
what we want to be. Nobody ever made a dollar out
of the fur trade by being nice to the Indians.

JOE BEEF:

Or to the animals.

MCGILL, MCTAVISH and MOLSON:
Or to the animals.

MCTAVISH:
10,141 foxes.

MCGILL:
11,141 minks.

MOLSON:
18,349 otters.

MCTAVISH:
19,286 bears.

MCGILL:
38,368 martens.

MOLSON:
137,558 beavers.

MCTAVISH:
And 1,144,439 raccoons died between 1793 and 1801
for the greater glory of the Montreal Northwest
Company.

MCGILL:
Fucking right.

MCTAVISH:
Fucking great.

CHIEF PEGUS lowers his mask and speaks.

CHIEF PEGUS:
My name is Chief Pegus of the Salteau tribe and I
remember when we used to hunt deer with bow and
arrow. It takes a long time to learn how to hunt the
deer. And then the white man brought us guns and
we forgot the old ways; we forgot how to plant corn,
we forgot how to weave our baskets and soon all we
could remember was killing the deer and the beaver

for their skins; and the white man pays us very little and lets us die when we are old.

MCTAVISH:

But I never lied to ye, Chief. I took ye for all I could get but I never lied to ye. I mean, I've never been a hypocrite, not like some of the Holy Rollers around here.

MCTAVISH glances at MOLSON.

CHIEF PEGUS:

We know you, Simon McTavish.

MCTAVISH:

Aye, ye know me, but ye didn't do much about it, did ye Chief? I mean ye could have whipped our asses but ye didn't and ye know why? 'Cause ye trusted us, ye believed every fucking thing we said and ye trusted us and look what it got ye, Chief, look what it got ye?

CHIEF PEGUS:

It's not over yet, McTavish.

CHIEF PEGUS exits.

MCTAVISH:

Aye, it's not over yet.

JOE BEEF:

Some of our modern day professors believe that the fur trade supplied one of the primary sources of capital, financing the entire Industrial Revolution, but what the professors don't tell you is that in some parts of Canada, nine-tenths of the Native population died producing that wealth — along with millions and millions of forest creatures.

MCTAVISH:

Bambi.

MCGILL:
    Bambi's mother.

MCTAVISH:
    Thumper.

MCGILL:
    Busy Beaver.

MCTAVISH:
    Chip and Dale.

MCGILL:
    Smokey the Bear.

MCTAVISH:
    Tweety Bird.

JOE BEEF:
    Dead, all dead.

MCTAVISH:
    Never, ever trust anyone, ever. Not even yourself.
    That's the secret of my success.

MCGILL:
    Aye, and we're rich now, eh Simon?

MCTAVISH:
    Aye, we're rich. Here, have a Molson's.

    MOLSON takes a pint out of his bible.

MOLSON:
    Cheers, for two hundred years.

MCGILL:
    Aye, I mean here we are now in our prime,
    honoured and respected by all.

MCTAVISH:
    Feared, ye mean — fear, not respect.

MCGILL:
Aye, I suppose.

MCTAVISH:
There's no supposing about it, James. It's fear that keeps us where we are and ye better not forget it for your own sake.

MOLSON:
Amen.

MCGILL:
Aye, aye, but are ye a happier man?

MCTAVISH:
Ye're getting soft, James McGill; soft, weak, flabby.

MCGILL:
Aye, but ye know, I think I was a happier man when I was making the money and now it's like the money is making me.

MCTAVISH:
So give it away if it bothers ye so much.

MCGILL:
I am.

MCTAVISH chokes on his beer.

MCTAVISH:
Ye're daft, man.

MCGILL:
I've made up a will leaving all my money to start a school.

MCTAVISH:
Going to name the school after yourself, of course.

MCGILL:
Aye, of course.

MCTAVISH:

>Ye're so modest, James, it's the thing about ye, I've always liked.

MCGILL:

>McGill University, I'll be immortal . . . immortal.

JOE BEEF:

>Ra-ra-rah-sis-boom-bah.

MCTAVISH:

>Molson, of course, is going to wait till charities become tax deductible. Am I right, John?

MOLSON:

>Blessed are the Poor in Spirit, for Theirs is the Kingdom of Heaven.

MCTAVISH:

>Ye tend to verge a wee bit on the sanctimonious, don't ye, Molson?

>*MCGILL nudges MCTAVISH.*

MCGILL:

>Simon, the contract.

MCTAVISH:

>Fuck him and his contract.

MCGILL:

>But the money, we need the money.

MCTAVISH:

>I don't need nobody, do ye understand me, James McGill? Nobody, is that clear? Am I making myself perfectly clear?

MOLSON:

>Wait, wait, I smell something?

>*MCTAVISH looks through the telescope.*

MCTAVISH:

> I see something. Look, over that way.

MCGILL:

> Aye, they're loaded right down to the waterline.

> *MOLSON stares with a handkerchief up to his nose.*

MCTAVISH:

> Aye, it's a good one this year, but who's that in the lead canoe with my nephew William McGillivray?

MCGILL:

> Who?

MCTAVISH:

> Why that's George Simpson, the chief factor of the Hudson's Bay Company.

> *VOYAGEURS enter paddling with SIMPSON and MCGILLIVRAY in the back carrying Hudson's Bay shopping bags full of fur skins.*

VOYAGEURS: *singing*

> Do your balls hang low
> Do they wobble to and fro
> Can you tie them in a knot
> Can you tie them in a bow
> Can you throw them over your shoulder
> Like you did a year ago
> Do your balls hang low?

MCGILL:

> They're drunk — they're all bloody well drunk.

JOE BEEF:

> The bar is open, boys.

> *VOYAGEURS go up to the bar.*

VOYAGEUR 1:

> Hey Joe, donne-moi une bière.

MCTAVISH:
> No drinking on the job.

MCGILL:
> No drinking.

VOYAGEUR 2:
> Aw, bise mon cul.

VOYAGEUR 1:
> We don't work for you no more, McTavish.

VOYAGEUR 2:
> Fucking right.

VOYAGEUR 1:
> Fucking gr-reat.

> *VOYAGEURS exit with their beers.*

VOYAGEURS: *singing*
> "I knew a girl from Montreal
> Could spread her legs from wall to wall
> But all she got was sweet fuck all
> From the Northwest company squadron"

MCTAVISH:
> What the hell is going on here?

MCGILLIVRAY:
> Greetings Uncle.

SIMPSON:
> Hello McGill.

MCTAVISH:
> What's he doing in our canoes, William?

SIMPSON:
> Ye mean, our canoes. We've bought you McTavish, the Northwest Company is now part of the Hudson's Bay.

MCTAVISH:
>A merger?

SIMPSON:
>No, a take-over.

MCTAVISH:
>What?

MCGILLIVRAY:
>Aye, it's true, Uncle. The big fish eats the little fish, eh?

MCTAVISH lunges for MCGILLIVRAY.

MCTAVISH:
>Ye son of a bloodsucker.

SIMPSON:
>Now listen, McTavish, ye know yourself that the competition was not good for business.

MCGILLIVRAY:
>Aye, Uncle, just look at the way the Voyageurs have been acting. Even the Indians have been getting uppity.

SIMPSON:
>We've got to stop this fighting amongst ourselves.

MCGILL:
>He's got a good point there.

MOLSON:
>A very good point.

MCTAVISH:
>Aye, well, you can shove it up your ass.

MCGILLIVRAY:
>But Uncle, ye've got no choices. We can't run things in the old way anymore. The days of Rugged Individualism are over, they're gone.

MOLSON:
>True — true.

>*SIMPSON hands MCTAVISH a pair of white gloves.*

SIMPSON:
>Here, McTavish.

MCTAVISH:
>What's this?

MCGILLIVRAY:
>It's the latest fashion, Uncle, gloves.

MOLSON:
>They keep your hands clean.

MCTAVISH:
>How much do I owe ye for these?

MCGILLIVRAY:
>Nothing. Compliments of the Bank of Montreal.

MOLSON:
>A what? A bank.

SIMPSON:
>Capital investment, Mr. Molson. A divine inspiration that will pay us dividends here on earth and in heaven above.

>*SIMPSON hands MCGILL some gloves.*

SIMPSON:
>Are ye with us, McGill?

>*MCGILL looks at MCTAVISH and then starts putting on the gloves.*

MCGILL:
>Aye, and you McTavish?

MCTAVISH throws the gloves at them.

MCTAVISH:
>Just fuck off, fuck yourselves and stay fucked. That's all I've got to say.

JOE BEEF:
>I couldn't have put it better myself.

MCGILLIVRAY:
>You're a loser, Uncle, a loser.

MCTAVISH goes to the bar.

MCGILL:
>Well, lads, now that we have a bank, what do we do with it?

SIMPSON:
>Investments, Mr. McGill, investments.

MCGILLIVRAY:
>Yes, we are on the verge of building a canal, nine miles long, twenty-eight feet wide, with seven locks each a hundred feet long and twenty feet wide.

MOLSON:
>How much is that going to cost us?

SIMPSON:
>Oh, about four hundred and forty thousand dollars.

MCGILL:
>Four hundred and forty thousand dollars?

MOLSON:
>That is rather a tidy sum.

MCGILLIVRAY:
>Don't worry about it, Mr. Molson.

MOLSON:
>Oh, I do, I do.

MCGILLIVRAY:
>Well, don't, don't.

SIMPSON:
>Yes, oh ye men of little faith, you must look ahead.
>You must look beyond your next dollar. You must
>plan for the future, our future, gentlemen, when this
>canal, these factories, this slum, this place called
>Pointe Saint Charles built on top of the City dump
>will make us rich . . . Rich . . . RICH, beyond our
>wildest wet dreams.

>>*They all quiver with excitement.*

MCGILL:
>Money.

MCGILLIVRAY:
>Money.

MCGILL, MCGILLIVRAY, MOLSON and SIMPSON: *together*
>Money.

>>*singing as they turn to exit.*

>Oh Oh Oh
>Jesus saves his money at the Bank of Montreal
>Jesus saves his money at the Bank of Montreal
>Jesus saves his money at the Bank of Montreal
>Jesus Saves Jesus Saves Jesus Saves

>>*They exit as MCTAVISH pulls away from the bar
>>with a bottle.*

MCTAVISH:
>Well, McGill has got a street and a school named
>after him and so does Simpson. And the Molsons,
>well you've still got them alive and doing well in this
>town today, making money out of ye. And me, well I

built myself a mansion away up there on the mountain out of sight and sound of all those bloody church bells. And then what happened? Oh, yeah, I died; died there of the booze at the age of fifty-two or was it fifty-four? No matter, but there's a plaque up there now saying I was this and that and a very honourable citizen, but it's all bullshit. I was a mean, tough, rotten son-of-a-bitch and even I was glad when I died. But at least I was never a hypocrite and ye can remember me for that, Joe Beef.

JOE BEEF:

Personally, I wouldn't piss on ya if you were on fire.

MCTAVISH:

Now that's what I would have liked for my epitaph.

Exits making the sound of bagpipes.

JOE BEEF:

Ya know we've got to be more careful about who we let into this country . . . yeah, and those guys with the weird accents weren't fooling around. By 1825, they finished the Lachine Canal, and by 1830, the boys were pulling in over a million dollars a year in toll receipts. A million bucks!

ALLAN enters dressed in a black cape, wearing a stovepipe hat, white gloves, and carrying a cane.

ALLAN:

And that's when I came to town.

JOE BEEF:

Sir Hugh Allan of the Allan Steam Ship Line.

ALLAN:

It was I that first put together the modern concept of a trans-Atlantic fleet based here in Montreal, with ships carrying goods over to Europe on a regular weekly basis and hauling back to Canada a particular commodity that was in great demand at that time.

JOE BEEF:
> Immigrants.

ALLAN:
> Yes, immigrants.

> *Three IRISH WOMEN enter wearing plaided shawls*
> *around their heads and shoulders.*

WOMEN: *singing*
> "Come back Paddy Reilly from over the sea
> Come back Paddy Reilly to me
> The grass it grows greener
> Round Bally James Duff
> Come back Paddy Reilly to me"

> *The WOMEN stand facing the audience.*

WOMAN 1:
> The potato crops failed three years in a row with the
> smell of the decay coming in from the fields.

WOMAN 2:
> We ate our pigs, our seedlings, the herbs and wild
> berries in the woods.

WOMEN: *together*
> And then we began to starve.

WOMAN 3:
> The children and the old people died first.

WOMAN 1:
> And the British landlords forced us off our farms
> because we could not pay the rent.

WOMAN 2:
> And a million died between 1846 and 1851 and
> another million emigrated.

ALLAN:
> Ireland was grossly overpopulated anyhow, and
> who's to blame for that?

WOMAN 1:

In 1847, a hundred thousand refugees came to
Canada, crowded on board the lumber transports.

WOMAN 2:

Fever Ships we called them, coffin ships with little
food or ventilation.

WOMAN 3:

And half the survivors of the voyage were sick or
dying as the first ships came up the Saint Lawrence
in the spring of that year.

WOMAN 1:

You could hear the Irish women keening for their
dead all up and down the water.

WOMEN: *together*

And many of those ships were yours, Sir Hugh
Allan.

ALLAN:

Those ships were made for loading lumber, they
weren't designed for passenger comfort. And besides,
I made the fares cheap enough, didn't I? Well, didn't I?

> *IRISH WOMEN keening as a DOCTOR enters in
> white smock with stethoscope and a GENTLEMAN
> in bourgeois costume, the same as Sir Hugh Allan's.*

GENTLEMAN: *in thin, almost effeminate voice*

Mr. Allan, we have been delegated by the Board of
Trade of the City of Montreal to speak to you about
your company's policy of leaving dead and dying
immigrants on the docks of this city.

ALLAN:

They pay for their passage to Montreal. I supply the
passage as per contract. I am within my rights.

GENTLEMAN:

Perhaps legally, but morally, Sir Hugh?

ALLAN:

Gentleman, I trust that the honourable members of
the Board of Trade are not here to discuss morality?

DOCTOR:

No, Sir Hugh, but your life and the life of your
family is in as much danger as the rest of ours from
this fever.

GENTLEMAN:

Not to mention the effect on the tourist trade.

DOCTOR:

Some of the immigrants have crawled into the City.
The danger of infection grows with every hour.

GENTLEMAN:

And we have an order from the Mayor that forbids
any more importation of immigrants, I'm afraid, into
Montreal.

ALLAN:

But I am not importing them. I am only transporting
them.

DOCTOR:

We are also under orders to place all ships under
quarantine.

ALLAN:

Quarantine? For how long?

DOCTOR:

For as long as it takes to examine the victims, sir.

GENTLEMAN:

But don't worry, Sir Hugh, the Board of Trade will
subsidize all extra expenses.

ALLAN:

Do we have that in writing?

DOCTOR:
> Do we?

GENTLEMAN:
> Ah, yes, yes, of course.

> *ALLAN looks at the paper.*

ALLAN:
> Very well gentlemen, I would appreciate it if you would commence immediately with your examination because the British Empire needs lumber and I am endeavouring to supply them with it.

GENTLEMAN:
> Certainly, Sir Hugh and now, Doctor?

> *The GENTLEMAN and the DOCTOR approach the IRISH WOMEN with kerchiefs up to their noses.*

DOCTOR:
> Yes.

> *The DOCTOR addresses the IRISH WOMEN.*

DOCTOR:
> Hello, I'm Doctor Foster of the Montreal Board of Trade and I want all of you who can walk to form a line in front of me, please.

> *The GENTLEMAN ushers the IRISH WOMEN into a single line.*

GENTLEMAN:
> Line up for the doctor, please.

DOCTOR:
> Everyone who can walk. You can all walk, that's good.

> *He examines the first woman.*

DOCTOR:

>   Open your mouth please . . . aaaaah . . . the sheds.

>   *Fist woman moves to the right as the DOCTOR
>   examines the second woman.*

DOCTOR:

>   Open please . . . the sheds.

>   *Second woman moves to the right as the DOCTOR
>   examines the third woman.*

DOCTOR:

>   Open . . . the sheds . . . the sheds. All of them to the
>   sheds. Now, are there any more on board who can walk?

GENTLEMAN:

>   Any more? . . . no, just the dying.

DOCTOR:

>   Very well, then, let's transfer these people.

WOMAN 1:

>   Fever sheds. A hundred feet long, fifty feet wide on
>   the river banks of Pointe Saint Charles.

WOMAN 2:

>   Twenty-two sheds with fifty people dying, a day,
>   throughout the long hot summer of 1847.

WOMAN 3:

>   And you could hear the cries of the people and smell
>   the fever in the City when the wind was blowing east.

>   *WOMEN keening as the DOCTOR approaches and
>   proceeds to use the WOMEN as lecture specimens.*

DOCTOR:

>   Typhus is transmitted by the common body louse,
>   which lives on human blood. The bite of the louse is
>   extremely irritating. The victim scratches, the skin is
>   broken and microscopic organisms called Rickettsia

51

attack the small blood vessels of the body, especially those of the skin and brain. Then as the temperature of the victim rises, he or she begins vomiting and developing agonizing sores as the body swells up, taking on a dark, congested hue which gives Typhus its Irish name of the Black Fever.

GENTLEMAN:
This way, please, all of those who can walk — this way.

The GENTLEMAN and DOCTOR escort the IRISH WOMEN offstage. The WOMEN keening.

JOE BEEF:
Over six thousand people died and were buried that summer in Pointe Saint Charles; shoved in a hole, like garbage, by the City Fathers of Montreal. Gone, forgotten and buried in a common grave.

ALLAN steps forward.

ALLAN:
Well, they brought it on themselves, didn't they? And how do we know it was six thousand that died? Maybe it was six hundred. And how do we know they were Irish? Maybe they were Jews? And, besides, I object to the characterization of me in this play and I know my family will too. And, believe me, they're still very much alive and doing well in this town, thank you very much.

JOE BEEF:
You better believe it.

ALLAN:
I mean it wasn't as if I was just a one-dimensional figure in a propaganda piece, I was a human being. I had feelings, I had hopes and dreams. But most of all, I had Me. Hit it boys.

Other BOURGEOIS enter in identical bourgeois costumes, joining ALLAN in a vaudeville style song and dance.

ALLAN: *singing to the tune of "Tea for Two"*
Because . . .
First there's me
And then there's you
And what you need
Is not for me
Because you see

CHORUS:
There's always you and me-ee

Shuffle-shuffle-shuffle

ALLAN:
There's nothing that I will not take
I know that's how to operate
And never give a sucker an even break

CHORUS:
That's a mistake

Shuffle-shuffle-shuffle

ALLAN:
There's she and he
And me makes three
And they and we are companies
But don't forget

CHORUS:
I'm always there for me-ee

Shuffle-shuffle-shuffle

ALLAN:
They and we and she and me
But most of all
I'm here for me

CHORUS:
That's Capital M and Capital E
And when I say Free, it's always for me

And the American Way is here to stay
For me

ALLAN:
That's me

CHORUS:
I'm me

*The BOURGEOIS all bang down their canes in
unison as JOE BEEF gongs a big frying pan. The
BOURGEOIS form a semi-circle.*

JOE BEEF:
Okay, now, before I ask the big question of the
evening, does anybody want a beer out there? Last
chance for a beer before I ask the big question. Okay,
are you ready? Are you ready? . . . Have you figured
out who the bad guys are yet?

*The BOURGEOIS lift their black capes up to their
eyes like vaudeville villains.*

BOURGEOIS:
Mee-Yuh-Ha-Ha-Ha-Ha-Ha.

JOE BEEF:
The guys in the black hats? Well that's true and its
not true. Because sometimes you got the good guys
doing the wrong things and the bad guys doing the
right things, and sometimes you got no Right or
Wrong — "It's just life and life only."

BOURGEOIS:
And the Law of Life is to live.

JOE BEEF: *reading from the "Communist Manifesto."*
"And the bourgeoisie cannot exist without constantly
revolutionizing the instruments of production and
thereby the relations of production and with them the
whole relations of society. All fixed fast frozen
relations, with their train of ancient and venerable

prejudices are swept away. All that is solid melts into the air. All that is holy is profaned. And man is at last compelled to face with sober senses, his real conditions of life, and his relations with his kind." *Puts down the 'Communist Manifesto' pamphlet and looks at the BOURGEOIS and then at the audience.* Ah yes, the Montreal bourgeoisie — a cute, cuddly little bunch, aren't they? But you know, there was a time, believe it or not, when those guys right here, the guys in the black hats, were a progressive force, a revolutionary force coming out of the British, American and French revolutions with Liberty, Equality, Fraternity and the belief that all men . . .

BOURGEOIS:
Not women.

JOE BEEF:
. . . all men are created equal and the best of them really believed that, no shit, they really did. But there's nearly always a big difference between what people want and what they get.

BOURGEOIS:
"Between the idea"

JOE BEEF:
"And the reality"

BOURGEOIS:
"Between the motion"

JOE BEEF:
"And the act"

BOURGEOIS:
"Falls the shadow"

JOE BEEF:
But every once in a while the who, what, where, when and why of it all comes together.

ALLAN taps his cane on the floor.

ALLAN:

Fellow companions, I now declare the Montreal chapter of the Royal Arch Millionaires Club open in due form. And Mr. J.J.C. Abbott, the Mayor of Montreal will now proceed to discuss a topic which concerns all of our interests and endeavours. Mr. Abbott . . .

All the BOURGEOIS tap their canes on the floor as ABBOTT proceeds to the front and faces the audience in a speaker's pose.

ABBOTT:

Thank you, Mr. Allan. Fellow companions, old winter is once more upon us and our inland seas are a dreary and inhospitable waste to the merchant. The splashing wheels are silenced, the roar of steam is hushed, the gay saloon so lately thronged with busy life is now but an abandoned hall. The animation of business is suspended and the life blood of commerce is curdled and stagnant in the Saint Lawrence, the great Aorta of the Frozen North.

JOE BEEF takes off his apron.

JOE BEEF:

I'm going for a shit.

He exits.

ABBOTT:

In Canada, blockaded and imprisoned by Ice and Apathy, there is no escape, but far away to the South is heard the daily scream of the steam whistle, the shaking noise and deafening sound of driving steel, fuming smoke and cinders as it rolls along at the incredible speed of twenty to thirty miles an hour into the Future. Gentlemen, I am talking about the Steam Locomotive.

BOURGEOIS 1:
>Too expensive.

BOURGEOIS 2:
>Where are we to get the materials?

BOURGEOIS 1:
>And besides, we already have our steamships.

BOURGEOIS 2:
>Yes, and we've already laid out millions, gentlemen, millions of dollars connecting the Rideau and the Lachine Canals.

ABBOTT:
>Yes, gentlemen, but meanwhile America has opened up the Isthmus of Panama while England is breaking through that of the Suez and planning grand trunk lines from Calais to Calcutta, and everywhere, gentlemen, one subject and one subject only rules the public mind: Railways.

ALLAN:
>Railways

ABBOTT and ALLAN:
>Railways.

BOURGEOIS 1:
>Bankruptcies.

BOURGEOIS 2:
>Bankruptcies.

BOURGEOIS 1 and 2:
>Bankruptcies.

ABBOTT:
>Gentlemen, we are practical people and we live in an eminently practical age, therefore, we must perforce admit to ourselves that not only has American export

by the Saint Lawrence ceased altogether but transit
privileges have been afforded over American routes
to Ontario.

BOURGEOIS 1:
I do not admit that.

ALLAN:
Then, sir, you do not admit to the facts.

ABBOTT:
And the fact is, gentlemen, that Toronto is exporting
and importing through her inland ports at such a rate
as threatens to reduce your City . . .

BOURGEOIS: *together*
Our City?

ABBOTT:
. . . your City to the position of a country town, a
mere trading post for a few miles of horseshit.

BOURGEOIS: *together*
Never-never.

ABBOTT:
Montreal, call it horseshit gentlemen, unless a
decision is drawn quickly that our fortunes and the
continuing success of our enterprises depend upon —

ALLAN and ABBOTT:
Railways.

BOURGEOIS 1:
Rubbish, it's too much.

BOURGEOIS 2:
We could very well over-extend ourselves.

BOURGEOIS 1:
Remember the panic of 1844.

BOURGEOIS 2:
> And the Americans.

BOURGEOIS 1 and 2:
> Aye, the Americans.

ABBOTT:
> Yes, it is true that the Americans do seem to have the edge on us, but let us not forget our most precious commodity, the one most single element that promises to make Montreal a world metropolis — Cheap Labour.

BOURGEOIS: *together*
> Cheap Labour.

ABBOTT:
> The Irish with their potatoes and maybe a bottle of booze, *(laughter)* and the French Canadians with their priests and their peasoup *(laughter)* are the cheapest labour in this country and together we can even make it cheaper.

BOURGEOIS: *together*
> Huzzah-Huzzah.

ABBOTT:
> But being cheap labour is not enough anymore. The Factory System demands a transformation of human nature.

BOURGEOIS:
> Amen.

ABBOTT:
> The working rhythms of the labourer must be methodized until the man is adapted to the discipline of the machine.

BOURGEOIS:
> Amen.

ABBOTT:
>His impulses must be controlled and his energies channeled if civilization is to progress.

BOURGEOIS:
>Amen.

ABBOTT:
>And who are the instruments of Progress?

BOURGEOIS:
>The Capitalists.

ABBOTT:
>And what is their function?

BOURGEOIS:
>To make profit.

ABBOTT:
>And what is profit?

BOURGEOIS:
>Unpaid labour.

ABBOTT:
>Therefore, wages must be kept down to a minimum.

BOURGEOIS:
>Amen.

ABBOTT:
>And whosoever believeth in this shall have everlasting Capital.

BOURGEOIS: *raising their arms*
>Hallelujah.

>>*ABBOTT blows on his whistle as JOE BEEF returns to his bar.*

ABBOTT:
    Workers.

> *Three WORKERS shuffle in to the front, facing
> ABBOTT and the audience. They move and talk in a
> mechanical fashion.*

ABBOTT:
    Ah, good morning, workers and how are you feeling
    today?

WORKER 1:
    Cheap.

WORKER 2:
    Cheaper.

WORKER 3:
    Cheapest.

ABBOTT:
    Very good and what are the signs of cheap labour?

WORKER 1:
    See.

WORKER 2:
    Hear.

WORKER 3:
    Speak no Evil.

ABBOTT:
    Your motto?

WORKERS: *together*
    Ignorance is Bliss.

ABBOTT:
    Your ambition?

WORKERS:
    To suffer.

ABBOTT:
    And the Commandments?

WORKERS:
    Thou shalt love thy boss as thyself. Thou shalt
    believe in him and obey his commands. Thou shalt
    not think, thou shalt not feel or ever go on a strike or
    ask for a raise for thine own sakes, amen.

ABBOTT:
    And do you believe?

WORKERS:
    We believe.

>   *ABBOTT raises his cane like a conductor's baton and
>   the WORKERS begin singing to the tune of the "Old
>   Rugged Cross."*

WORKERS: *swaying as they sing*
    Oh, the old factory boss
    So despised by the world
    Has a wonderful attraction
    For me

BOURGEOIS: *swaying in counter rhythm in the back*
    For you

WORKERS:
    And I love my old boss
    With my dearest and best
    Although it means suffering
    And shame

BOURGEOIS:
    And shame

WORKERS:
    But I'll cherish my old factory boss

BOURGEOIS:
    Factory boss

WORKERS:
    I will starve while he gets rich and fat

BOURGEOIS:
    Rich and fat

WORKERS:
    I will work for the old factory boss

BOURGEOIS:
    Factory boss

WORKERS:
    Till one day I just lay down and die

BOURGEOIS:
    Lay-down-and-die

    ABBOTT taps his cane on the floor.

ABBOTT:
    Thank you workers, and now gentlemen, each of
    these specialized labour unions . . .

    The BOURGEOIS gasp.

BOURGEOIS:
    Unions?

ABBOTT:
    . . . Freudian slip, gentlemen. I meant to say that
    each of these specialized labour units . . .

    The BOURGEOIS sigh in relief.

ABBOTT:
    . . . is standardized, interchangeable and anxious to
    conform to whatever commands we give them. It's
    called, Inner Direction.

BOURGEOIS:
> Inner direction?

ABBOTT:
> Yes, they do what they're told because they want to.

BOURGEOIS 1:
> But, how well will they do it?

ABBOTT:
> Well, what do you want gentlemen? Give me an
> order.

ALLAN:
> A railway.

BOURGEOIS: *together*
> Yes, railways, railways.

ABBOTT:
> Very well. *Points his cane at the worker like a magic
> wand.* Newtonian physics plus Adam Smith, minus
> the Communist Manifesto equals — The Grand Truck
> Railway.

> > *WORKERS transform themselves into a steam
> > locomotive.*

BOURGEOIS:
> The G-T-R

ABBOTT:
> A monogram of almost mystical portent for all
> Montrealers as westward the Star of Empire takes its
> course in the form of an indestructible artery of steel.

ALLAN:
> Power.

ABBOTT:
> Power.

BOURGEOIS: *together*
>Power.

ABBOTT:
>Flowing out of Montreal like a huge generator. *He blows his whistle.* All aboard.

>*The train, lead by the WORKERS starts to move.*

ALLAN:
>How long will it take us to get to Toronto, Abbott?

ABBOTT:
>Oh, about ten hours.

ALLAN:
>Just ten hours, my God, do you know what this means?

BOURGEOIS 1 and 2:
>Do you know what this means?

ALLAN:
>Our whole concept of Time and Space is changing, J. J.

ABBOTT:
>Railway time.

WORKERS:
>Time.

ALLAN:
>And this is just the beginning.

BOURGEOIS: *together*
>Just the beginning.

ALLAN:
>"Forward, forward, let the great world spin forever down the ringing grooves of Change."

>*The train chugs offstage.*

BOURGEOIS:
    Whoo-whoo.

WORKERS:
    Whoo-whoo.

BOURGEOIS:
    Cheap . . . labour . . . cheap . . . labour . . . labour
    . . . cheap . . . labour.

    They exit.

JOE BEEF:
    "Forward, forward, let the great World spin forever
    down the ringing grooves of Change." Who said
    that? Tennyson said that, Lord Alfred fucking
    Tennyson and they really did believe that kind of
    shit, ya know. They really did believe they could go
    on forever as Pointe Saint Charles down here in the
    southwest corner of Montreal became the Industrial
    Heart of Canada with over twenty thousand people
    working in the flour mills.

    WORKERS enter stage left and right.

WORKERS 1 and 2:
    Iron mills.

JOE BEEF:
    Saw mills.

WORKERS 3 and 4:
    Shoe factories

JOE BEEF:
    Sugar refineries

WORKERS 1 and 2:
    Textiles.

JOE BEEF:
    Abbatoirs.

WORKERS 3 and 4:
>Freight yards.

JOE BEEF:
>Doing twelve hours a day for a dollar a day, six days a week.

WORKER 1:
>Packing.

WORKER 2:
>Wrapping.

WORKER 3:
>Stacking.

WORKER 4:
>Bagging.

JOE BEEF:
>No bulldozers in those days, just bull labour.

WORKER 1:
>Me, its my knee. The left one; kind of pulls to the side.

WORKER 2:
>Me, its my arm. Right here in the shoulder.

WORKER 3:
>Me, its my back. Been bothering me for months.

WORKER 4:
>And me, I'm just getting older.

WORKERS: *together*
>We're all getting older.

>*WORKERS continue work motions.*

JOE BEEF:
>And it was around that time that I first opened "Joe Beef's Canteen," right down here by the waterfront.

WORKER 1:
Nickel a beer and all you can eat, eh Joe?

JOE BEEF:
All ya can grab, ya mean. But ah, it wasn't bad, ya know. Better than being in the Army. Yeah, that's how I got out of Ireland—by fighting in the Crimean War. Ya know, yours is not to reason why, yours is but to do and die, and die, and die we bloody well did. *Takes a shot of Irish whiskey.* Figured I'd get a little peace and quiet once I opened this place, but no. Found myself in another war right here in Pointe Saint Charles.

ABBOTT and ALLAN enter stage left and right.

ABBOTT: *blows a whistle*
Step on it men!

The WORKERS begin laying down track as they exit in a line.

WORKER 1:
"And drill ye tarriers, drill"

WORKERS 2, 3 and 4:
"And drill ye tarriers, drill"

WORKERS: *together*
"For its work all day
For sugar in your tay
Down along the railway

WORKER 1:
"And drill ye tarriers, drill"

WORKERS 2, 3 and 4:
"And blast"

WORKER 1:
"And fire"

WORKERS 2, 3 and 4:
"And blast"

WORKER 1:
"And fire"

WORKERS exit.

JOE BEEF:
Work-work-work. Christ, pretty soon they'll be having ya doing it with your dicks!

ABBOTT:
Ah yes, and that railway did increase our rate of profits as the Molsons, the Redpaths, the Allans, the Drummonds and the Abbotts all moved up on the hill into Westmount, claiming our place in the sun.

ALLAN:
Ah yes, it was a time when I built myself a thirty-four-room mansion with a ballroom and greenhouse right on the very edge of the mountain, far out of the smoke and stink of Pointe Saint Charles. I called it Ravenscrag. You call it the Allan Memorial Hospital.

ABBOTT:
It was a time when the middle-class man was confident that his country was safe from invasion, his investments protected and that the woman he married would stay by his side for the rest of his life, as his property, like the British Empire, continued to expand.

JOE BEEF:
It was a time when Pointe Saint Charles had the highest TB rate in North America and one out of every four children died before the age of two.

ALLAN:
And of course a lot of people died, but people are always dying. I mean, do you know what it takes to build a city? Do you?

ABBOTT:

By buying cheap and selling dear, we have created a world of continuous and accelerating material and moral progress.

ALLAN:

Based on Natural Selection.

ABBOTT:

Survival of the Fittest.

ALLAN:

Supply and Demand.

ABBOTT:

Character and Duty.

ALLAN:

Self-Help.

JOE BEEF:

And Murder.

ALLAN:

The procedures, gentlemen, the procedures. We need not worry about the dimension.

ABBOTT:

A ten percent profit will ensure our interest in any venture.

ALLAN:

Twenty percent will make us positively eager.

ABBOTT:

For fifty percent, we will betray our most sacred promises.

ALLAN:

And there is not a crime we would not commit.

ABBOTT:
>Or a law that we would not break for . . .

ALLAN and ABBOTT:
>One hundred percent profit . . . and we mean
>Business.

JOE BEEF:
>If you got hundreds, you got hundreds. If you got
>thousands, you got thousands. But if you got
>millions, you got Murder.

ALLAN:
>That's what it takes to make Progress.

ABBOTT:
>But it's nothing personal.

WORKERS:
>Nothing personal.

ALLAN and ABBOTT:
>If it wasn't us, it would be somebody else.

WORKERS:
>It it wasn't us, it would be somebody else.

WORKER 1: *singing in a chanting voice*
>"Hello, my name is Joe
>I got a wife, a dog and a family
>I work, in a button factory
>One day, the boss comes up to me and says
>Hey Joe, are ya busy?
>I said no
>Turn the wheel with your right hand, Joe"

>>*All the WORKERS start moving their right hands in
>>unison.*

WORKERS 1 and 2:
>"Hello, my name is Joe
>I got a wife, a dog and a family

I work, in a button factory
One day, the boss comes up to me and says
Hey Joe, are ya busy?
I said no
Turn the wheel with your left hand, Joe''

All the WORKERS start moving both hands in unison.

WORKERS 1, 2 and 3:
"Hello, my name is Joe
I got a wife, a dog and a family
I work, in a button factory
One day, the boss comes up to me and says
Hey Joe, are ya busy?
I said no
Turn the wheel with your head, Joe''

All the WORKERS start moving their heads in unison with both their hands and singing in an exasperated tone of voice.

WORKERS 1, 2, 3 and 4:
"Hello, my name is Joe
I got a wife, a dog and a family
I work, in a button factory
One day, the boss comes up to me and says
Hey Joe, are ya busy?
I said'' - Strike!

The WORKERS all raise their fists and singing the "International," they step forward.

WORKERS and JOE BEEF:
"It's the last call to battle
Close the ranks, each in their place
The Worker's International
Shall be the human race
It's the last call to battle
Close the ranks, each in their place
The Worker's International
Shall be the human race''

WORKERS cheer as DARLINGTON steps forward

DARLINGTON:
>Fellow workers, we refuse to take a wage cut of twenty percent or ten percent or any percent.

JOE BEEF:
>That's right.

Cheers from the WORKERS.

DARLINGTON:
>We want a nine-hour day, regular two-week payments and an end to the truck system. No more paying us with company goods.

JOE BEEF:
>Go get them.

Cheers from the WORKERS.

DARLINGTON:
>We demand that the authorities recognize our Union and we won't go back till they meet our demands — all of them.

LEPINE steps forward, joining DARLINGTON.

LEPINE:
>Les Blokes and les Pepsi's toute ensemble.

WORKERS: *together*
>Strike-Strike-Strike

LEPINE:
>Moi, c'est Al Lepine and this is Bill Darlington and together we helped organize the men in the Lachine Canal Strike.

DARLINGTON:
>We were both Knights of Labour who believed that

Labour creates all wealth, therefore all wealth belongs to the workers.

LEPINE:
And that an injury to one is an injury to all.

WORKERS: *together*
Une Grande Union.

DARLINGTON:
We were out six bloody weeks fighting off the cops.

LEPINE:
The newspapers they called us scum and saboteurs.

DARLINGTON:
A threat to Democracy.

JOE BEEF:
Their Democracy.

DARLINGTON:
By the end of the first week, we were hungry.

LEPINE:
By the end of the second week, we were starving.

DARLINGTON:
No worker's compensation, no unemployment insurance, no welfare. All we had was Joe.

WORKERS:
Joe Beef.

LEPINE:
Joe, he fed us for six weeks; six semaines.

DARLINGTON:
A thousand workers and their families.

WORKERS:
Men, women and children.

JOE BEEF:
"The man who cheats his workers is no man at all.
The worker has his rights."

WORKERS:
The worker has his rights.

WORKERS: *chanting*
We want more pay
We want more time
That's why we're on a picket line
They point at JOE BEEF
Pick it

JOE BEEF and the WORKERS do a song and dance
number to the tune of "I Walk The Line."

JOE BEEF: *singing*
I keep a close watch on the picket line
I keep my eyes wide open all the time
The way the cops harass us is a crime
Don't cross the line

WORKERS:
This job is mine

JOE BEEF:
As sure as they are wrong
And we are right
We've got to hold our line
Both day and night

WORKERS:
We want our jobs
And so we've got to strike

JOE BEEF:
Make up your minds

WORKERS:
Don't cross the line

JOE BEEF:
>I find it very very easy
>To be rude
>To company finks and rats
>And stoolies too
>And I admit
>That I don't give a shit

WORKERS:
>You cross that line

JOE BEEF:
>Your ass is mine
>You cross the line

WORKERS:
>Your ass is mine

JOE BEEF and the WORKERS recite the following:

JOE BEEF:
>Yeah, and there's those that will
>And those that won't

WORKERS:
>Those that do
>And those that don't

JOE BEEF:
>But draw the line
>And you will find

WORKERS:
>It's black and white

JOE BEEF:
>It's day and night

WORKERS:
>You want your rights

JOE BEEF:
>
> You've got to strike

WORKERS:
>
> Don't waste your time with talk and rhyme

JOE BEEF:
>
> Just kick their ass
> And they'll learn fast

WORKERS:
>
> Not to fink
> And not to rat

JOE BEEF:
>
> And never ever be a scab

WORKERS and JOE BEEF:
>
> The scabs crawl in
> The scabs crawl out
> They crawl in under
> And all about
> They crawl in early
> They crawl in late
> They crawl right under the factory gate

WORKER 1:
>
> S

WORKER 2:
>
> C

WORKER 3:
>
> A

WORKER 4:
>
> B

WORKERS and JOE BEEF:
>
> SCABS!

DARLINGTON:

> But you know, fellow workers, it's the unions
> themselves that do the worst scabbing: unions
> scabbing on each other and it's even worse today.

LEPINE:

> And you guys got to do what we did. You've got to
> have your strike meetings and talk about the time for
> solidarity.

DARLINGTON:

> The need to organize the whole working class.

LEPINE:

> The need to organize one big union.

WORKERS:

> Solidarity.

LEPINE:

> Yeah, Solidarity, one big fucking union.

DARLINGTON:

> And in six weeks we got the support of other
> workers, of other unions.

LEPINE:

> The yard workers.

DARLINGTON:

> The rail workers.

LEPINE:

> The truckers.

DARLINGTON:

> The freighters.

WORKERS: *together*

> And all the other workers.

LEPINE:

Organizing day and night.

DARLINGTON:

Who does what and where and how.

LEPINE:

The money.

DARLINGTON:

The food.

LEPINE:

The transportation and you know, pretty soon, we began to see that maybe we don't need the bosses. We can do all this ourselves. We don't need them to fuck up our lives.

WORKERS:

This is our City.

LEPINE:

We don't need Westmount.

WORKERS:

We can do it ourselves.

LEPINE:

And for six semaines, my friends, there was no murder. There was no crime, there was no hunger in Pointe Saint Charles.

WORKERS:

No hunger in Pointe Saint Charles.

A SOLDIER begins marching up the center aisle towards the WORKERS.

SOLDIER:

Gotta dig . . . gotta dig . . . gotta dig . . . dig . . . dig . . . dig . . . Etc.

LEPINE:

> And it was becoming more than just a strike. It was becoming something we didn't know. Something that we never heard about. And some guys said there was going to be a revolution and we were joining to take over the government. We were going to get rid of the bosses, but how do we do that?

> *SOLDIER marching in place in front of the picket line.*

JOE BEEF:

> Ya gotta move before they do.

WORKERS:

> We gotta move.

JOE BEEF:

> Ya gotta go all the way.

WORKERS:

> We gotta go all the way.

JOE BEEF:

> Ya gotta throw the first fucking punch.

WORKERS: *raising their fists*

> We . . . Gotta . . . Throw . . . The . . . First . . . Fucking . . . Punch.

> *ALLAN and ABBOTT take their front positions to the left and right of the WORKERS, facing the audience*

ALLAN and ABBOTT:

> Soldiers of the Prince of Wales Brigade . . . Stand to.

> *The SOLDIER stands ready.*

JOE BEEF:

> And I don't know about the other guys, but I was scared shitless. I really was.

ALLAN and ABBOTT:
>Ready.

The SOLDIER stands ready.

JOE BEEF:
>And I tried talking to the guys and I know what it's like when the man says aim and you aim, and the man says fire and you fire. But they didn't want to do it. I could tell by their eyes.

WORKERS:
>We are your brothers.

JOE BEEF:
>Don't tell it.

WORKERS:
>We are your sisters.

JOE BEEF:
>Don't do it.

ALLAN and ABBOTT:
>Aim.

The SOLDIER aims.

WORKER:
>No.

ALLAN and ABBOTT:
>Fire.

WORKERS:
>No.

ALLAN and ABBOTT:
>Fire.

The WORKERS back up.

WORKERS:
No.

ALLAN and ABBOTT:
FIRE.

SOLDIER *stamps his foot in simulation of firing as the WORKERS lower their fists.*

JOE BEEF:
And the line was broken.

DARLINGTON:
Our biggest strike.

LEPINE:
Our best chance.

WORKERS: *together*
Our best chance.

JOE BEEF:
1887.

WORKERS:
Lachine Canal Strike.

JOE BEEF:
1905.

WORKERS:
Canadian Pacific Strike.

JOE BEEF:
1919.

WORKERS:
Winnipeg General Strike.

JOE BEEF:
1949.

WORKERS:
>   Canadian Seaman's strike.

JOE BEEF:
>   Mille neuf cent soixante et douze.

WORKERS:
>   Grève Générale du Québec.

JOE BEEF:
>   1986.

WORKERS:
>   Gainers.

JOE BEEF:
>   And we could have won.

WORKERS:
>   We don't have to live this way.

JOE BEEF:
>   We could have won.

WORKERS:
>   We don't have to live this way.

ALLAN and ABBOTT:
>   Soldiers of the Prince of Wales
>   Brigade . . . Dismissed.

>   *SOLDIER turns around and marches away down the
>   center aisle.*

ALLAN:
>   And now, Mr. Abbott, we'll negotiate.

ABBOTT:
>   Yes. Now workers, you may not want to believe this,
>   but we recognize most of your suffering. We accept
>   most of your grievances, we understand your urges
>   for self-improvement and we are ready to compromise.

ALLAN:
>Because we can afford to.

ABBOTT:
>And because it's good business.

ALLAN:
>And good business means profit and progress for us
>all.

ABBOTT:
>Naturally, we cannot accept this illegal strike, but we
>are ready, in the interests of social harmony . . .

ALLAN:
>And expanding economy . . .

ABBOTT:
>To encourage and promote the idea of
>respectable . . .

ALLAN:
>Very respectable . . .

ABBOTT:
>Legal . . .

ALLAN:
>Very, very legal . . .

ABBOTT:
>Craft Unions. And to that purpose, we have invited
>Samuel Gompers, President of the American
>Federation of Labour here for a discussion on the
>subject. Mr. Gompers . . .

ALLAN:
>Sam? Where's that sweet-talking Sam?

ABBOTT:
>Will Sam Gompers please come to the head of the
>factory. Sam?

GOMPERS, *a big guy in a loud suit, smoking a big cigar, makes his way up the center aisle to the front.*

GOMPERS:
Right here, boys, a gomp-gomp-gomp, so what's the problem here, huh? We got a problem?

ABBOTT:
The men here wish to organize a union.

GOMPERS:
Oh, ya do, huh? Well, better forget all that injury to one is an injury to all crap, because from now on it's every union for itself. Gomp-gomp-gomp.

ALLAN and ABBOT:
A gomp-gomp-gomp.

GOMPERS *begins talking to both the audience and the WORKERS on the picket line, but addresses himself basically to the audience.*

GOMPERS:
But only for the skilled workers, ya get me? The broads, the niggers and the frogs can all go fuck themselves, a gomp-gomp-gomp. Because all that one big union bullshit is just one big Commie pinko plot to take over our country and destroy our precious rights and liberties. *Places his hand over his heart and sings,* "America, America, God" — hey, come on you guys, don't ya know the words?

ABBOTT:
Um, Mr. Gompers, this is Canada.

GOMPERS:
Canada? Well, same thing, ain't it? A-gomp-gomp-gomp.

WORKERS:
A-gomp-gomp-gomp.

85

GOMPERS:
Okay, all you skilled workers to the front.

ALLAN and ABBOTT:
English workers only.

Two of the WORKERS step forward.

JOE BEEF: *yelling*
Scabs.

GOMPERS:
Never mind that foreign agitator, just raise your
hands and repeat after me: A-gomp-gomp-gomp.

WORKERS 1 and 2 raise their left hands.

WORKERS:
A-gomp-gomp-gomp.

GOMPERS:
That's your left hand, stupid.

WORKERS:
That's your left hand, stupid.

GOMPERS: *shrugging*
Okay, okay, I believe in the American Way.

WORKERS:
I believe in the American Way.

GOMPERS:
And I will support the Profit System.

WORKERS:
And I will support the Profit System.

GOMPERS:
Even if I have to scab.

WORKERS:
>Even if I have to scab.

GOMPERS:
>A-gomp-gomp-gomp.

WORKERS:
>A-gomp-gomp-gomp.

>>*GOMPERS and WORKERS begin to sway in rhythm.*

GOMPERS:
>A Fair Day's Wages for a Fair Day's Work

WORKERS:
>A Fair Day's Wages for a Fair Day's Work

GOMPERS:
>A Fair Day's Wages for a Fair Day's Work

WORKERS:
>A Fair Day's Wages for a Fair Day's Work

>>*GOMPERS and WORKERS singing and dancing.*

GOMPERS:
>'Cause I'm a hard-hat worker

WORKERS:
>I'm a hard-hat worker

GOMPERS:
>I'm a Union-pay worker

WORKERS:
>I'm a Union-pay worker

GOMPERS:
>And I don't think
>And I don't care
>I just spend my money

And get fat on beer
'Cause I'm a hard-hat worker

WORKERS:
I'm a hard-hat worker

GOMPERS:
I'm a Union-pay worker

WORKERS:
I'm a Union-pay worker

GOMPERS:
And I hate all the niggers
And I hate all the frogs
'Cause they want my pay
And they want my job
'Cause I'm a hard-hat worker

WORKERS:
I'm a hard-hat worker

GOMPERS:
I'm a Union-pay worker

WORKERS:
I'm a Union-pay worker

GOMPERS:
I just sit at home
And turn the TV on
'Cause I'm alright, Jack
I don't need no flack
I don't sing the blues
'Cause I paid my dues
And it's a one-two
A one-two-three
Sen-ior-ity Forever

WORKERS and GOMPERS:
Sen-ior-ity Forever

Sen-ior-ity Forever
'Cause the Union keeps us — In

JOE BEEF:
Scabs.

GOMPERS:
It's in the contract.

JOE BEEF and WORKERS 3 and 4:
Scabs.

WORKERS 1 and 2:
It's in the contract.

GOMPERS:
Yeah, that's right, boys, you're getting it, you're getting it. Now let's go down to the Union Hall and sign you guys up, for a price of course.

WORKERS 1 and 2:
For a price of course.

GOMPERS:
A-gomp-gomp-gomp.

WORKERS 1 and 2:
A-gomp-gomp-gomp.

GOMPERS and WORKERS 1 and 2: *exit, singing to the tune of "Oh Tannenbaum."*
The working class can kiss my ass
I got the foreman's job at last
The working class can kiss my ass
I got the foreman's job at last

ABBOTT:
Thank you very much, Mr. Gompers. And now the French workers will line up to receive Communion from Bishop Bourget.

BISHOP BOURGET enters followed by TWO NUNS who are chanting.

NUNS:
My Mother Plays Dominoes Better Than Your Mother Plays Dom-om-i-nos.

WORKERS:
No, she doesn't

NUNS:
My Mother Beat Your Mother In The Dominoes Championship in Vancouver Last Year.

WORKERS:
She che-ee-eated.

NUNS: *threatening the WORKERS with their rules.*
Down on your knees, down on your knees, down on your knees.

The WORKERS go down on their knees.

NUNS:
They are now in a position of worship, Your Grace.

BOURGET:
Very well, I will now address the Faithful.

NUNS: *announcing*
The Monseigneur Bishop Bourget will now address the Faithful.

BOURGET: *facing the audience*
My children, it saddens me to see you here today in this place, in this City, in this Babylon of Iniquity and Sin. Yes, it is not natural, this factory life, this city life. It leads to temptation.

NUNS:
Temptation.

BOURGET:

It leads to abomination.

NUNS:

Abomination

BOURGET:

My children, why do you leave the clean air of our villages for such a place? Why do you leave behind the Catholic joys and decencies of the farm life for a slum street in Pointe Sainte Charles, why?

WORKER 1:

Shit and mud, that's why.

WORKERS: *yelling as they get up from their knees.*
Shit and mud, shit and mud, shit and mud.

NUNS: *threatening the WORKERS with their rulers.*
Down on your knees, down on your knees.

WORKERS get back down on their knees.

WORKER 2:

We ask only for justice, Monseigneur. They are cutting our wages.

BOURGET:

Ask not for justice, my son, but pray for forgiveness. Pray.

NUNS:

Pray-pray-pray.

BOURGET:

And remember my children, that we are to accept depravation and misfortune here on earth. Indeed we must welcome humiliation and pain if we want to live in everlasting peace and joy in the hereafter. So I ask you, my children, are a few years of sordid lust and gluttony worth an eternity of suffering?

WORKERS: *getting up off their knees*
Yeah-yeah.

JOE BEEF:
You're fucking right.

> *NUNS threatening the WORKERS with their rulers.*

NUNS:
Down on your knees, down on your knees.

> *WORKERS get back down on their knees.*

BOURGET:
My children, your souls are in danger, your very
souls.

NUNS: *announcing*
The Monseigneur Bishop Bourget will now give the
Communion.

> *BOURGET passes out the communion wafers to the
> WORKERS who stick out their tongues.*

BOURGET:
Our Father who art in Heaven, bless these sad,
misguided workers and keep them happy on the
Holy Minimum Wage for the own sakes.

NUNS:
Amen.

BOURGET:
Help them to remember that all authority comes from
God and that our Holy Mother Church represents the
power of God in the land of Quebec
where . . . *(chanting)* nothing must die and nothing
must change.

NUNS:
Nothing must change.

BOURGET: *making the sign of the Cross*
> Now rest in peace. Work, my children. Don't
> complain and make plenty of babies 'cause that's
> your lot in life, Lalanya.

NUNS:
> "I can't blame ya"

BOURGET:
> "Lalanya"

> *BOURGET exits followed by the chanting NUNS.*

WORKERS:
> Eat my body and drink my blood . . . eat my
> body . . . and drink . . . my blood . . . eat . . . my . . .
> body . . . and . . . drink . . . my . . . blood

> *WORKERS still on their knees as ALLAN and*
> *ABBOTT take center stage.*

ABBOTT:
> Ah, yes, and by 1889, less than fifty men living
> within one square mile of Montreal owned and
> controlled over half the wealth in Canada.

ALLAN:
> A vast and mighty empire that was beyond Good
> and Evil. An empire that required a new breed of
> men who would starve the flesh.

ABBOTT:
> Expose the bone.

ALLAN:
> Define the will.

ABBOTT:
> Restrain the senses.

ALLAN:

Scorn all talk of Mercy for we have nothing for the
outcast and the unfit. Let them die in their misery.

ABBOTT:

Stamp down on the wretched and the weak.

ALLAN:

This is the Law of the Strong.

ABBOTT:

This is our Law.

ALLAN:

And the Joy of the World.

ABBOTT:

The Joy of the World.

ALLAN:

And even though we're dead and in our graves, we
still have control over you. We still run this country.
We made this country.

ABBOTT:

The Hudson's Bay Company.

ALLAN:

The Bank of Montreal.

ABBOTT:

The CPR.

ALLAN:

The CNR.

ABBOTT:

The Royal Bank.

ALLAN:

Montreal Trust.

ABBOTT:
>Sunlife Assurance.

ALLAN:
>We profit from everything.

ABBOTT:
>Nothing can stop it.

ALLAN:
>War or no War.

ABBOTT:
>Peace or no Peace.

ALLAN and ABBOTT:
>We-Always-Profit.

>>*Other bourgeois enter behind ALLAN and ABBOTT*
>>*who proceed to lead the group in a song-and-dance*
>>*number.*

ALLAN: *singing to the tune of Dylan's "Serve Somebody"*
>Now you may call it Francs
>Or you may call it Yen
>You may call it Pounds
>Or you may call it Pence

ABBOTT:
>Cash and carry

ALLAN:
>Cheque or Charge

ABBOTT:
>And Credit to your number

ALLAN:
>You're in the black

ABBOTT:
>But sooner than that

ALLAN and ABBOTT:
　　The Interest drags you under

ALLAN:
　　And you're gonna pay somebody

ABBOTT:
　　Yes indeed

ALLAN and ABBOTT:
　　You're gonna pay somebody

BOURGEOIS: *chorus*
　　Pay somebody

ALLAN:
　　And it might be in silver
　　Or it might be in gold
　　But you're gonna pay somebody

BOURGEOIS: *chorus*
　　Pay somebody

ALLAN:
　　Now it might be filthy lucre
　　It may be bones or bucks

ABBOTT:
　　Some call it the root of all evil

ALLAN:
　　It could be a shot in the dark

ABBOTT:
　　Just spin the wheel of fortune

ALLAN
　　But you can't pass Go till you start

ALLAN and ABBOTT:
　　Paying somebody

BOURGEOIS: *chorus*
>Yes you are

ALLAN and ABBOTT:
>You're gonna pay somebody

BOURGEOIS: *chorus*
>Pay somebody

ALLAN:
>And it might be an IOU
>Or it might be a loan
>But you're gonna pay somebody

BOURGEOIS: *chorus*
>Pay somebody

ABBOTT:
>Now you might be a fisherman
>Or you might be a farmer
>You might be a factory hand
>A stevedore, a barber

ALLAN:
>You may dance and you may dream

ABBOTT:
>Be a saint or be a sinner

ALLAN:
>Think a lot or drink a lot

ABBOTT:
>Be fat or thin or bitter

ALLAN:
>But you're gonna pay somebody

BOURGEOIS: *chorus*
>Yes you are

ALLAN and ABBOTT:
>You're gonna pay somebody

BOURGEOIS: *chorus*
>Pay somebody

ALLAN:
>And you might not like the prices
>Or appreciate the rates
>But you're gonna pay somebody

ABBOTT:
>Yes you are

ALLAN and ABBOTT:
>You're gonna pay somebody

BOURGEOIS: *chorus*
>Pay somebody

ALLAN and ABBOTT:
>Pay somebody

ALLAN and ABBOTT and BOURGEOIS: *chorus*
>And that somebody is US!

>>*ALLAN, ABBOTT and the BOURGEOIS all bang their canes down on the floor simultaneously while staring at the audience.*

ALLAN and ABBOTT: *laughing like vaudeville villains*
>Mee-yuh-Huh-Ha-Ha-Ha-Ha-Ha

>>*They begin exiting, followed by the BOURGEOIS.*

BOURGEOIS: *chorus*
>Mee-yuh-Huh-Ha-Ha-Ha-Ha-Ha

ALLAN and ABBOTT:
>We Always Profit

>>*They exit.*

JOE BEEF:

And the rest is rock-and-roll history. I mean we lost
then and you're still losing today, with the rich up
on the mountain and you down here in the Pointe
with your twenty-five percent unemployment and
your fucking ceiling falling down around your ears.
And it's you that built this City. It's you that made
them rich. You made them filthy fucking rich and
what have ya got, eh? Nothing. You got nothing and
you're going to stay nothing until you learn to throw
the first fucking punch. Are ya listening? Do you
hear me? Naw, what do you know, eh? What do you
care. Ya always forget anyhow. Ya don't remember.
Ya always forget.

He pours himself a shot of whiskey at the bar.

WORKERS 1 and 2: *singing as they get up from their knees.*
"Have Thy own way, Lord
Have Thy own way"

*Other WORKERS come out on stage joining in the
song.*

WORKERS:
"Thou art the power
I am the Slave"

WORKERS:
"Bend me and shape me
After Thy Will
While I am waiting
Yielded and still"

DARLINGTON:
Joe Beef died on January the fifteenth, 1889, of a
heart attack, at the age of fifty-four.

LEPINE:
And there he was, ya know, lying there on the
sawdust floor in the bar and somebody goes and gets
the priest — that Father Nolan there — and he comes

running. Hurry up, Father, dépêchez-vous . . . Jose
Beef is dying. And the priest comes running with all
that holy water and says any last words my son?
Any last words?

JOE BEEF:
Yeah. Fuck off.

LEPINE:
"Fuck off," and he did. Father Nolan, I mean.

DARLINGTON:
But we gave Joe one hell of a funeral.

WORKERS:
Thousands of us following the coffin in the streets.

DARLINGTON:
No priests, no preachers, no politicians, just us.

WORKERS:
On a cold, cold January day, Joe.

DARLINGTON:
Me and Al Lepine were asked to do the eulogy.

WORKERS:
Remembering you, Joe.

DARLINGTON:
I think I said the usual things. I mean, I had to keep
it short.

WORKERS:
'Cause we were all freezing our asses off, Joe.

DARLINGTON:
But Al was good. You spoke good that day, Al.

LEPINE:
Aw, I was half drunk, maybe more than half.

WORKERS:

'Cause we had a last beer at your place, Joe.

LEPINE:

I think I started to cry.

JOE BEEF:

He was always fucking crying.

LEPINE:

Hey, so would you after twelve beers. But me, aw, you know, he was a good guy that Joe. He was a good guy. Hey, we all know he had his moods, heh?

WORKERS:

Yeah-yeah.

LEPINE:

But when there was nobody else, nobody, he was there for us, heh? Backing us when we needed him there in that big strike, making sure we all got something to eat, some place to sleep. He was there for us and we don't forget that, Joe.

WORKERS:

Joe Beef

LEPINE:

And we won't forget what you said about throwing that first punch. Always throw the first punch, that's what Joe said and he's right. We've got to learn to throw the first punch, especially now.

WORKERS:

In the nineties.

LEPINE:

No more waiting till they kick us in the teeth before we do anything, my friends. Oh no, we've got to do it first, do it fast and do it hard if we want to beat the bosses. And we can do it, we can win. We can beat them only if we stand together.

101

WORKERS:
Stand together.

LEPINE:
Only if we're strong together.

WORKERS:
Strong together.

LEPINE:
Because just like these fingers on my hand . . . *(holds up his hand)* Like this, we are nothing. But this . . . *(closes his hand into a fist)* we are Everything.

WORKERS:
Une grande union.

LEPINE:
Une Grande Union.

TOGETHER:
Une Grande Union.

> *JOE BEEF comes out from behind his bar as the WORKERS bring on a replica of the Black Rock Memorial Stone.*

JOE BEEF:
We took a seventeen-ton boulder that we dredged out of the river and hauled it to shore. A huge black rock like a bad tooth, pulling it out of the water. We chained and wedged and wheeled it over and placed it on top of the common grave.

> *The WORKERS place the replica of the Black Rock center stage, then gather around it in a semi-circle.*

JOE BEEF and WORKERS: *reading out the inscription carved on the Black Rock*
"To Preserve from Desecration, the Remains of 6,000 immigrants who died of Ship Fever, A.D. 1847. This Stone is erected by the Workers of Peto, Brassey and

102

Betts, employed in the construction of the Victoria Bridge, A.D. 1859.''
They raise their fists.
Je Me Souviens

JOE BEEF:
The bar is open.